NORTHBOROUGH COUNTY SCHOOL

PETERBOROUGH

726

S

E

W

N

18

14

19

20

D1632563

726

A Ladybird Book
Series 649

There have been parishes and parish churches in Britain for about 1,200 years. A parish church is like a book, telling the story of the Christian faith and the lives, joys and sorrows of the people who, over the years, have met there to worship.

This Ladybird book tells you the meaning of, and the reason for, so many of the things you will see there.

J3.

What to look for
INSIDE A
CHURCH

by P. J. HUNT
with illustrations by
RONALD LAMPITT

Publishers: Ladybird Books Ltd
Loughborough
© Ladybird Books Ltd
(formerly Wills & Hepworth Ltd) 1972
Printed in England

The Parish Church

Our country is divided into parishes and each parish has its own church, often many hundreds of years old. No two churches are quite the same, but there are certain things which are common to all of them. You will read about these in the following pages, as well as about some of the rarer items which you will not find in every church.

Each church has its clergyman, who may be called a rector or a vicar or a priest-in-charge. Sometimes a group of clergymen look after a group of parishes, and assistant curates help them in some of the busier places.

Many of the old parish churches are extremely beautiful buildings. In many ways they also record the lives of their parishioners over the centuries—the births, achievements, marriages and deaths—and the bequests of those who lived in the parish.

The churches being built today, in new towns and housing estates, are often more modern in style but equally interesting.

0 7214 0304 2

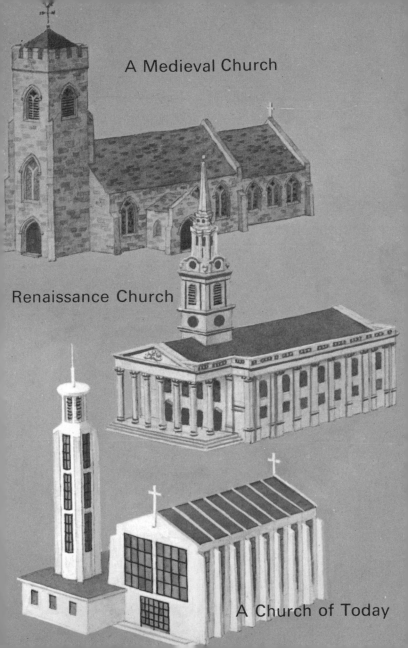

A Medieval Church

Renaissance Church

A Church of Today

Pews and bench-ends

Pews are fixed benches on which people sit. Once there were no seats in churches and the congregation stood or knelt.

Later, in some churches, a few seats were attached to the wall for old and sick people, and from this comes the saying, 'The weakest go to the wall'.

Fixed seats for all the people were introduced about the 15th century. Later, the squire and wealthy patrons of the church had their private pews, often near the chancel, and owners of large houses had benches reserved for their families and households.

Benches were sometimes surrounded by high, box-like structures to keep out the draughts, and sometimes were replaced by comfortable armchairs and cushions. Even curtains and a stove were sometimes added inside the box structure.

15th century wood-carvers often finished the tops of bench-ends with a decoration known as a poppy head (from the French word 'poupée'—a puppet or figure-head). Sometimes these bench-end tops were carved with figures, scrolls, animals or the arms of the family who owned the pew—often very beautiful examples of wood-carving.

You may also find carved panels at the ends of some benches.

Bench-end—Wygenall St. Mary, Norfolk.

A Bench-end
Top and Panel

Stalls and misericords

Stalls are the fixed seats in the chancel where the choir and clergy usually sit. Until the Reformation (a great religious revolution which took place about the 16th century), most churches had some wooden stalls which were separated from one another by projecting elbows.

In cathedrals and sometimes in large churches, you may find panelling at the back of the stalls and canopies overhead; these often go up to a great height and are beautifully carved. They are not usually found in smaller churches.

Some choir-stalls have hinged, tip-up seats, and if you lift these up you will probably find a shelf-like projection underneath carved with all sorts of quaint figures and scenes from everyday life. These are called *misericords*, from a Latin word meaning 'pity' or 'compassion'. In medieval times, long services were held during which the priests and monks had to stand; the misericords could be used as rests to support aged and infirm men as they stood through the services.

The wood-carvers let their imagination go on these carvings and some of their work is most amusing. You may find kitchen scenes, hunting scenes or even someone suffering from toothache—with his finger pointing to the bad tooth! They carved the subjects they knew in their daily life.

Choir-stalls and misericord detail
—Christchurch, Ludlow, Shropshire.

Stalls *showing seats tipped up and shelf-like projections (misericords)*

A Misericord

The altar and reredos

The *altar* is the most sacred part of the church, and it is here that Christians come during the Holy Communion service. It stands in a railed-off part of the church called the sanctuary.

The altar is usually, but not always, at the east end of the church, and is placed where all can see it. Until the Reformation, the altar was generally made of stone. In early days a saint's body was sometimes buried under it; later the relics of a saint were sometimes inserted in the 'mensa' or top.

After the Reformation, the stone altar was replaced by a table which was brought out into the chancel (*see No. 1 on the inside front cover*) so that people could gather round it. This is being done in some modern churches.

The space between the top of the altar and the window-sill above may be enriched with a *reredos*. This may be of wood, stone or alabaster and is often beautifully carved or painted. Sometimes it has niches containing figures of saints. Where the niches are empty, it is probably because the figures were destroyed at the time of the Reformation.

Sometimes you may also see embroidered curtains at the back and sides of the altar, and these help to add to its dignity and beauty.

Altar—Footscray Church, Essex.

The Altar and Reredos

Lecterns and Litany desks

The *lectern* is the desk on which rests the Bible. It is usually of brass or wood and is moveable. Wooden lecterns are mostly in the form of a desk with two, or occasionally four, flat sloping sides. Brass lecterns are usually in the shape of an eagle or pelican with outstretched wings. The bird often stands on a ball, which represents the world, while the Bible on the bird's back symbolises the Gospel being carried on wings to the corners of the earth.

In some places you may see evidence that a Bible has been chained to the lectern. In 1536, King Henry VIII ordered that a Bible be placed in every church and at that time English Bibles were so rare that they were in great danger of being stolen. Sometimes they were kept in a locked Bible box for safety.

The *Litany desk*. This is the prayer desk which you may see in the centre aisle of some churches. At this the priest says the Litany—an 'asking' prayer in which the people take part. Its place in the nave of the church, where the people sit, reminds us that priest and people join together in prayers, such as the Litany, for the needs of the world.

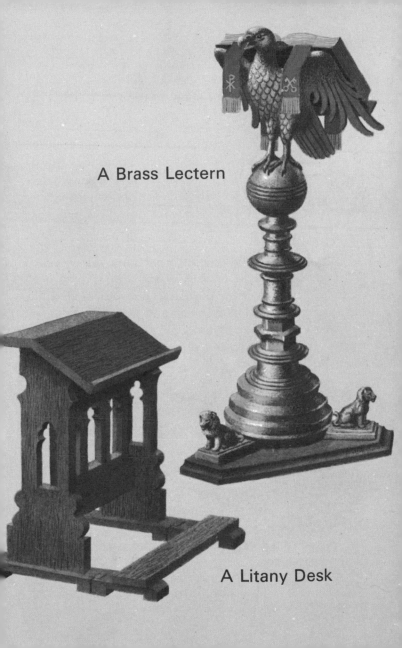

A Brass Lectern

A Litany Desk

Fonts and font covers

You will almost always find the *font* near the church door. It is a large bowl-shaped object which holds the water used in baptism.

In early days, fonts were large enough to allow adults to stand in them and be completely immersed. Nowadays only a little water is sprinkled on the candidate's head, and baptism usually takes place within a few weeks of a baby's birth. However, it can take place at any time of life.

Fonts are often of stone but sometimes you may find them made of marble or lead. Many are carved, sometimes with scenes from the Bible or pictures showing the sacraments such as Baptism and Holy Communion. Some very early fonts had weird figures carved on them, perhaps to symbolise the renouncing of evil through baptism.

Early fonts did not have covers, but in 1236 the Archbishop of Canterbury ordered fonts to be covered and locked so that superstitious people should not steal the holy water. Some covers are permanently fixed to the top of the font, and have a door opening as though to a cupboard.

In the 15th century, very large, richly carved wooden covers were used, and these were often of a great height and looked something like church spires. They needed a pulley and chain or rope to raise them.

Norman font—Burnham Deepdale, Norfolk.
Font cover—Ufford, Suffolk.

A Norman Font

An elaborate
Font Cover
on top of a Font

The pulpit

The *pulpit* is the raised, enclosed platform from which the preacher gives the sermon. In olden times there were no pulpits, and sermons were preached outside the church or in front of the altar, and later from the chancel. In 1603 it was ordered that pulpits be placed in all churches.

Today, you will usually find pulpits made of either wood or stone, most of the early ones being constructed of oak. They have several sides, and may be hexagonal (six-sided) or octagonal (eight-sided), with panels which are often carved or painted. Some stand on wooden stems while others are on stone platforms.

Early pulpits were moveable, and in the unheated churches of olden days it was the custom to move them to the least draughty part of the building; as those were the days before the introduction of pews, it was easy for the people to move also.

Some pulpits have canopies or sounding-boards over them, so that the preacher's voice is carried more easily to the far end of the church.

When galleries were erected in churches in the 17th and 18th centuries, to provide extra seats for large congregations, three-decker pulpits were sometimes erected; in these, the preacher used the top part, the reader the next part, while the clerk sat in the lowest part.

The Pulpit

Screens

Between the *nave*, where the people sit, and the *chancel*, where the choir sits, you will often see a *screen*. In medieval times the chancel was used only by the clergy and their assistants, and the screen kept out other people—and their dogs too.

Screens are also used to separate chapels from the nave or chancel, and also to enclose tombs.

Early screens were of stone, but from the 14th and 15th centuries wood was used. The wooden screens were beautifully carved by skilled woodworkers, and often some of the lower panels were painted.

Upon some screens you may see a *rood-beam* over which is fixed a figure of Christ on the cross, called the *rood*. Usually figures of Mary, the mother of Jesus, and St. John are on either side of Christ.

The rood was a most important part of the church in the Middle Ages, and candles were erected on a candle-beam in front of the rood-beam. When these were lit, people's eyes were drawn to the rood as soon as they entered the church, because there was very little other lighting. In this way they were reminded of the Christ Whom they had come to worship.

The organ

Organs have been used from about the 10th century, and were to be found in very large churches by about the 13th century. In the 18th and 19th centuries, however, village orchestras sometimes led the music in smaller churches, the musicians playing in a gallery at the west end of the church. These galleries can still be seen in some churches.

An organ contains hundreds of pipes of all sizes. When the organist plays a note, air travels by means of bellows to a certain pipe. The air vibrates in the pipe, making a sound that may be anything from a high-pitched whistle to a deep, low-pitched note, depending on the size of the pipe.

The organist uses his hands on the two or three keyboards, and his feet on the pedal notes beneath the keyboard. The 'stops' beside the keyboards control the varieties of tone so that an organ may imitate various musical instruments, both wind and string. The stops have names, like 'diapason', 'vox humana', 'flute', 'celeste', etc.

The chief purpose of the organ in church is to lead the singing, not to replace human voices.

Many organs have elaborate wooden cases, and those of the 17th and 18th centuries were often especially beautiful, being richly carved and ornamented.

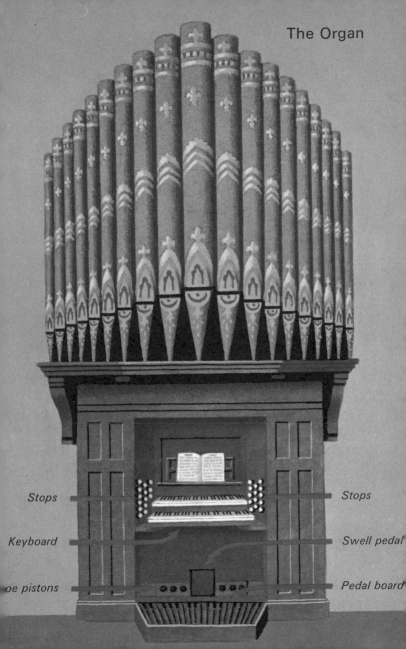

The Organ

Stops

Keyboard

oe pistons

Stops

Swell pedal

Pedal board

Sedilia and piscina

Sedilia are canopied seats on the south side of the chancel. Originally they were behind the altar, along the east wall which was curved in a semi-circle. Some modern churches are returning to this arrangement.

Some sedilia have two seats, others three, and a few have four. Usually the seats are of different heights; the highest, nearest the altar, is for the priest, the next for the deacon who reads the Gospel, and the third for the sub-deacon who reads the Epistle. When there was a fourth seat this was used by the clerk.

In some churches, you may find the sedilia designed jointly with the *piscina*. This is a shallow stone basin with a drain. It is used for washing the sacred vessels—the chalice (cup) and paten (plate)—after the Holy Communion service. The drain leads to the consecrated ground of the churchyard outside.

If you see a piscina in an aisle or transept (i.e., the 'arms' of any church which is built in the shape of a cross) or elsewhere, it usually means that there was an altar there at one time.

Sedilia and Piscina—Cherry Hinton, Cambs.

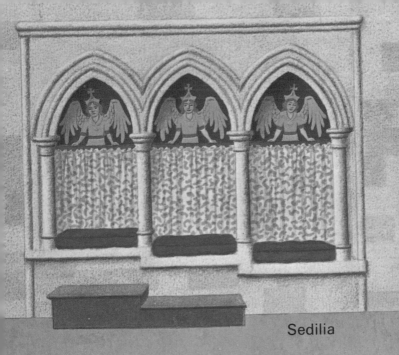

Sedilia

A Piscina

Alms boxes, dole cupboards and chests

Alms boxes. By 'alms' we usually mean the money offerings of the people. The earliest collection boxes were made from a hollowed-out piece of tree-trunk held together with iron bands. Nowadays you will still find boxes into which you may put money to help the work of the Church, both in that parish and beyond.

Dole cupboards. In the Middle Ages, rich people sometimes left money in their wills so that bread could be bought for the poor. This bread was kept in a dole cupboard, and was distributed to the poor people of the parish at the end of the Sunday service. Some dole cupboards were finely carved and most had ventilation holes in the door.

Chests. For hundreds of years large chests, with separate compartments, were used for the purpose of collecting alms. One compartment was for 'Peter's Pence'—a tax once paid to the Pope.

Chests were also used for keeping parish registers, accounts, wills and other records. These formed a most useful record of the births, deaths and activities of people living in the parish, and are still consulted by present-day historians. Some chests had three or more locks, each having a separate key kept by a different person. This meant that each person had to be present before the chest could be opened.

Old oak alms box—Blyth, Notts.
Dole cupboard—St. Albans, Herts.
Ancient iron chest—Warbleton, Sussex.

An old oak
Alms Box

A Dole
Cupboard

An ancient
Iron-Bound
Chest

Bequest boards, hatchments and mural paintings

Bequest boards. On the walls of the church, often in the porch, you may see bequest boards which tell of the gifts to charity which various people have made in the past. The amounts shown give us an idea of the changing value of money, and make fascinating reading.

Hatchments. A hatchment is a board which was carried in a funeral procession and was afterwards hung over the doorway of the dead person's house. It is usually about 4 feet square and has painted on it the arms, crest or motto of the dead person.

After it had been displayed at the house for a period, it was hung in the church, and you may still find hatchments there today. The colours used on the hatchment had various meanings to indicate the status of the person who had died.

Mural paintings. The inside walls of churches were often decorated with designs or paintings of biblical events; these helped to teach the people in the days before most of them could read. The paintings also helped to make the church more beautiful.

Unfortunately most of these paintings were whitewashed over by the Puritans, but in some churches the whitewash has been carefully removed so that the beauty of the old paintings can be seen once more.

Bequest board—Ashchurch, Kent.
Hatchment—Oxford.
Mural painting—Chichester.

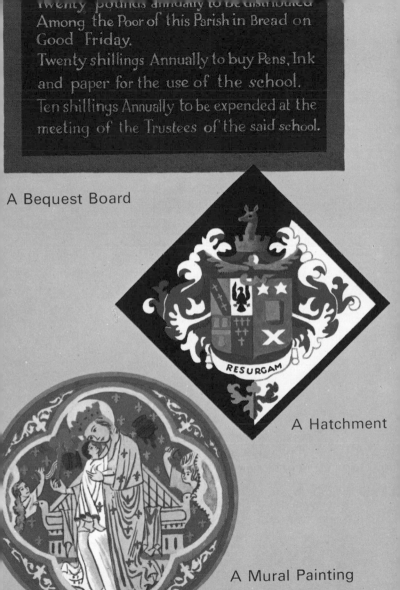

Twenty pounds annually to be distributed
Among the Poor of this Parish in Bread on
Good Friday.
Twenty shillings Annually to buy Pens, Ink
and paper for the use of the school.
Ten shillings Annually to be expended at the
meeting of the Trustees of the said school.

A Bequest Board

RESURGAM

A Hatchment

A Mural Painting

Effigies

Very early tombs were simple stone slabs over a grave, but in the 13th century an *effigy* (image) of the dead person was often carved on top of the slab. Many tombs were shaped like a box and had a life-sized effigy lying on the top. Sometimes effigies were of carved and painted wood.

Effigies have taught us much about costume, armour and heraldry, and we may often get an idea of the date of the tomb by looking at these details.

In the 14th century, stone canopies were often placed over the tombs and were sometimes masterpieces of carving in marble, alabaster or stone.

On the church walls there may be memorial tablets, from which we can learn something of the styles of lettering used at various periods.

Round the sides of a tomb you sometimes see several small figures. These probably represent the dead person's family and are called 'weepers'. You may also see some fine wrought-ironwork in the railings surrounding a tomb.

A knight's helmet and other parts of his armour were sometimes carried in his funeral procession and afterwards placed in the church; you may still find them in some churches.

Effigies—Goudhurst, Kent.

Painted Wooden Effigies

Stone coffins, brasses and ledger stones

Stone coffins. In the early Middle Ages wealthy people were buried in stone coffins, and sometimes these were let into the church floor so that the top of the coffin formed part of the paving.

The coffin itself was formed from a solid block of stone, having a long space, narrowing at one end, for the body and a circular space at the other end where the head rested. The body itself was wrapped either in grave clothes or in some other form of dress.

Brasses. These are thin pieces of metal or 'latten' let into the stone and forming part of the pavement of a church. They were introduced into this country during the 13th century as memorials to people who had died. They are often engraved with a figure but this is not usually intended to be a portrait of the dead person. Many brasses are in memory of aristocrats and titled people who fought in the Crusades and who owned large estates, or of merchants who helped to pay for extensions to the church.

Ledger stones. In some churches you will see carved floor slabs in a greyish blue stone. These are ledger stones and usually they have an inscription in very beautiful lettering, with a coat of arms above it. They became popular when brass-making declined.

Ledger stone and stone coffin—Eynesford, Kent.
Brass—Trumpington, Cambs.

Here Lyeth Interr'd
the Bodyes
of
S.ʳ HENRY BOSUILE Kᵗ,
of Little Mote Eynsford
And
Dame MARY his Wife
She Was Buried April ẙ 24ᵗʰ
ANNO DOMⁿ: J693
Aged 78
yeares.
He was Buried MARCH ẙ 18ᵗʰ;
ANNO DOMⁿ: J702
Aged 75
yeares.

Inscription and coat of
arms on a Ledger Stone

A Stone
Coffin

A Monumental
Brass

Cresset stones and hour-glasses

A *cresset stone* is a block of stone—or sometimes metal—which has several cup-shaped holes in it. These were filled with oil or grease and a wick floated on top. These cresset stones were used before other forms of artificial lighting were known, and gave light for people who had duties in the church during the hours of darkness.

A cresset is also the name for a fire-basket, which was sometimes placed on the top of the tower, particularly if the church was near the coast. When filled with burning wood or charcoal, the cresset acted as a beacon and could be seen for miles around. Such beacons were lit, for instance, at the time of the Spanish Armada, but after that period they gradually fell into disuse and there are very few about today.

An *hour-glass* is shaped rather like an egg-timer. Hour-glasses were used in churches to time the sermon and sometimes, in pre-Reformation days, to mark the time of Scripture readings. They were usually placed near the pulpit.

It is rare to find a complete hour-glass in a church these days, but you may sometimes still find the stand or bracket to which it was fixed.

Cresset stone similar to one in Brecon Cathedral.
Hour-glass similar to one at Compton Bassett.

A Cresset Stone

An Hour-glass

Stained glass

Stained glass has been used for hundreds of years to add beauty and colour to our churches. Often the windows show biblical scenes, and these helped to teach the people about their religion in the days when most of them could not read.

The separate pieces of glass each have their own colour and are set into strips of lead. Some of the finest stained glass dates from the 13th and 14th centuries and even earlier.

In the middle of the 16th century, craftsmen began painting the colours directly on the glass; this is called 'enamelling' and the result looks rather like oil painting.

The colours in early stained glass were each thought to have a meaning; for instance, red meant divine love, white—divine wisdom, yellow—faith, and so on.

Some people believed that the colours chosen for our Lord's robes were selected according to the period of His life shown in the picture. Thus people who understood the colours in this way could read more into the stained glass picture than just the scene it portrayed.

14th century window depicting St. Catherine—
Deerhurst, Glos.

A 14th Century stained glass window
depicting St. Catherine

Candles and banners

Candles. These were once the main source of light in churches, but nowadays most churches are lit by electricity.

When Christians were persecuted and driven underground into the dark catacombs in Rome, candles were very necessary. Their use today is partly a reminder of the Church's sufferings in the past. They also remind us that Christ is the Light of the World, and the two candles on the altar are sometimes thought of as symbols of the two sides of Christ's nature—the human and the divine.

Candles also add beauty to a church—especially if they are grouped as part of a candelabrum and their flickering lights reflect in the polished metal.

Banners. You will often see various sorts of banners in church. These are carried in church processions and are usually embroidered with pictures or sacred symbols. Church organisations often have their own banners, and you may see, for instance, a Sunday School banner or a Mothers' Union banner. There will also probably be a banner bearing a picture or symbol of the church's patron saint—i.e., the saint to whom the church is dedicated.

HOLY TRINITY

LAMORBEY

Candle
(actual height 4 ft.)

Banners

The stoup and the pyx

The *stoup*. This is a small niche containing a recessed basin just inside, or sometimes outside, the church door. It may be in one of the pillars nearest the door. It contains holy water which is blessed every Sunday.

Stoups are rather like piscinas (see page 22) but are often smaller and plainer and rarely have a drain. Also they are in a different part of the church from the piscina, which is usually in the chancel.

The holy water in the stoup is for use by worshippers entering the church. Some dip a finger in it and make the sign of the cross on their foreheads. This reminds them of their baptism and of their need to be cleansed from sin.

The *pyx*. This is a small box or casket in which is put the consecrated bread from the Holy Communion service. It is reserved there until it is taken to the sick and dying.

The pyx is usually made of costly materials, and in the church you may see it suspended in the chancel in front of the altar, or it may be kept in the aumbry, (see page 40).

Stoup—Bures, Suffolk.

A Stoup

A Pyx

Squints, the aumbry and the Easter sepulchre

Squints or hagioscopes. In some churches you will see an opening cut at an angle through the wall or pillar near the chancel arch. These openings were made so that people in the side aisles could get a clear view of the sanctuary and see the whole service of Holy Communion at the altar. Many of these openings have been filled up, plastered or boarded over but you may sometimes see where they have been.

Some churches had a squint in the room above the porch; this was probably for the use of the acolyte (the minister's assistant) who had to ring the sanctus bell at a certain time in the service.

The *aumbry.* A small cupboard in the church wall in which were stored the holy oils used for annointing very sick people. In medieval times, sacred vessels, relics and books were often kept in it.

The *Easter sepulchre.* This is a recess usually found in the north wall of the chancel. On Good Friday the host (consecrated bread) and a crucifix or cross were placed in this, and a watch was kept on them until Easter morning. They were then carried to the High Altar with great ceremony, to remind people of Christ's death and burial and of His resurrection.

Squint and aumbry cupboard—Lamorbey.

An Easter Sepulchre
(with Host and Crucifix)

A Squint

An Aumbry Cupboard

Sanctuary lamp, aumbry lamp, Bishop's chair and stool of repentance

Sanctuary lamps. These are lamps hung in the sanctuary in front of the altar. They are always lit and remind us that God is always present. Sometimes you will see one, sometimes three and sometimes seven.

One lamp is usually found in places where there is the Reserved Sacrament (the bread and wine from the Holy Communion Service for taking to sick people). Three lamps are to remind us of the three Persons of the Trinity. Seven lamps remind us of the seven gifts of the Holy Spirit,—i.e., wisdom, understanding, counsel, fortitude, knowledge, true godliness and the fear of the Lord.

An *aumbry lamp.* A lamp found near the aumbry (see page 40) to indicate that the sacred bread and wine are to be found there.

A *bishop's chair.* The special chair which stands near to the altar and which is placed at the entrance to the chancel for the Bishop to use when he takes a Confirmation Service.

A *stool of repentance.* These are not very common today. Originally, the stool was a low seat, sometimes called a frith stool, which was for use by anyone who had broken the law and had come to the church to seek sanctuary. Also guilty people were sometimes compelled to sit on it as a punishment for their sins.

A Sanctuary Lamp

An Aumbry Lamp

A Bishop's Chair

A Stool of Repentance
(or Frith Stool)

Emblems, monograms and symbols

If you look carefully, you will find various *symbols* in the carvings, embroideries and stained glass of the church. It is interesting to know what they mean.

It is said that early Christians did not think it reverent to write the names of God or Jesus in full, so they made various symbols for them. Here are some which you are likely to see:

Symbols of God the Father—A hand coming from a cloud, or a hand raised in blessing.

Symbols of God the Son, Jesus Christ—

XP=the first two letters of the Greek word for Christ (XPICTOC).

IHS or IHC=the first three letters of the Greek for Jesus (IHCOYC).

INRI=the initial letters of the Latin words for 'Jesus of Nazareth, King of the Jews' (IESUS NAZARENUS REX IUDAEORUM). This was the inscription which Pilate wrote and put on the cross (see John 19, v. 19).

A Ω=Alpha and Omega. The first and last letters of the Greek alphabet, thus signifying the beginning and the end. They remind us that Jesus is the beginning and the end of all things and suggest His everlasting nature (see Revelation 1, v. 8).

Symbols of God the Holy Spirit—A dove with a three-rayed nimbus (halo), or a sevenfold flame, as a symbol of the Holy Spirit's power (see Acts 2, v. 1-4).

God

Christ

Jesus

INRI

Jesus of Nazareth,
King of the Jews

Alpha and Omega

Symbol of God
the Holy Spirit

More symbols

It is interesting to find out to whom a church is dedicated and then to look around the church and see if you can find any symbols of that saint in carvings, embroideries or stained glass.

The church may have as its patron saint one of the four evangelists, St. Matthew, St. Mark, St. Luke and St. John, each of whom wrote a Gospel. You will find their books at the beginning of the New Testament, and in a church the symbols of these saints are often found as follows:

St. Matthew—a man; *St. Mark*—a lion; *St. Luke*—an ox; and *St. John*—an eagle.

You may also find crossed keys which are the symbol of *St. Peter*, reminding us of Christ's promise to him (see Matthew 16, v. 18-19); and also an X-shaped cross, which is the symbol of *St. Andrew*.

An open Bible (sometimes found in carvings or stained glass) is another symbol for the Word of God.

A ship represents the Church sailing through all perils. The word 'nave', meaning the part of the church where the people sit, comes from the Latin word 'navis', meaning 'a ship'.

A fish. This was originally a secret sign used by the early Christians when they were being persecuted. The initial letters of the Greek words for 'Jesus Christ, Son of God, Saviour' spell the Greek word for 'fish'; so by using this sign, Christians were declaring their faith to one another.

St. Matthew

St. Mark

St. Luke

St. John

St. Peter

An Open Bible

A Ship

A Fish

Liturgical colours

In many churches specific colours are used at certain times of the Church's year. You may see these colours in the hangings on the altar, the bookmarks for the Bible, Prayer Book and other service books, in the pulpit fall (the hanging from the pulpit desk), and in the stole—which is the long, narrow band of silk which a clergyman wears about his neck at sacramental services (e.g. Holy Communion and Baptism).

These colours are as follows:

Violet—the colour of penitence—during the seasons of Advent (the four weeks before Christmas) and Lent (the forty days before Easter, not counting Sundays), and also on days known as Vigils and Ember Days.

In some churches unbleached linen is used in Lent, and black on Good Friday.

White (or sometimes gold)—the festival colour—used on festivals such as Christmas, Easter, Ascensiontide and on some saints' days.

Red—the colour of fire and blood—used at Whitsuntide to remind us of the coming of the Holy Spirit to the disciples like tongues of flame, (see Acts 2, v. 1-11), and on festivals of martyrs—to remind us of their sacrifices.

Green—the colour of nature—used during the seasons of Epiphany and Trinity. This last season lasts for about half the year.

Liturgical Colours

Green
(Nature)

White
(Festival)

Violet
(Penitence)

Red
(Fire and Blood)

The Church's books

The Holy Bible. On the lectern you will see a large Bible from which are read the Lessons, or passages of Scripture, in public worship; you will also see Bibles in other parts of the church building. Some churches provide Bibles in the pews so that the people may follow the Scriptures whilst they are being read.

The Bible is not one book, but many. It contains sixty-six books altogether—thirty-nine in the Old Testament (telling of the time before Jesus Christ came to earth), and twenty-seven in the New Testament (telling the story of Jesus's life on earth and the beginnings of the Early Church after He had been crucified, and had risen to life again).

The Authorised Version of the Bible which is widely used was published in 1611, and only came to us after many people had suffered and died in order to get an English translation available for everyone.

Nowadays there are several versions of the Bible which are written in more modern English—one of the most popular is the New English Bible, the first edition of which was published in 1970, though the New Testament had been previously published in modern English in 1961.

The Book of Common Prayer. This is the Prayer Book of the Church of England and contains the order of most of the services held in church. It was published in 1662. The word 'common' in this sense means 'for everyone'.

Some modern services are now being tried, and for the most part these are published in separate little booklets.

Hymn-books. There are various hymn-books to be found in churches, and these contain hymns (sacred poems set to music). Hymns have always formed part of Christian worship.

The Holy Bible

The Book of
Common Prayer

CONTENTS